William Bolcom

Nine Bagatelles

for piano

Commissioned for the Van Cliburn
International Piano Competition

ISBN 0-7935-7854-X

EDWARD B. MARKS MUSIC COMPANY / EXCLUSIVELY DISTRIBUTED BY HAL•LEONARD® CORPORATION

7777 W. BLUEMOUND RD. P.O. BOX 13819 MILWAUKEE, WI 53213

Commissioned for the 10th Van Cliburn International Piano Competition by the William S. Davis Family
in honor of Eddie Maude Smyth, who represents the spirit and effort of all the Cliburn Competition volunteers

Nine Bagatelles

I

WILLIAM BOLCOM(1996)

NB: Accidentals obtain only throughout a beamed group: = all A♭

In music with key signature, traditional practice applies.

* *Chopin, Op. 33 no.4*
** *Bottom note remains A♮, even on a Bösendorfer.*

(...the ghost mazurka)

II

Rather slowly, but light; poco rubato (♩ = ca. 46)

Slow Mazurka

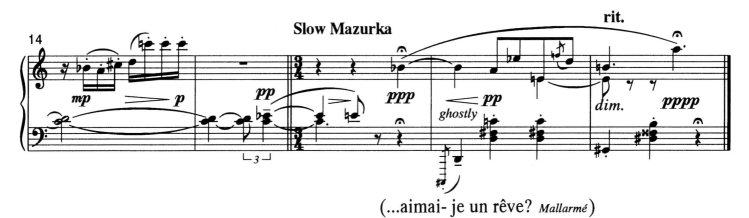

(...aimai- je un rêve? *Mallarmé*)

III

Fast, but spacious; senza tempo

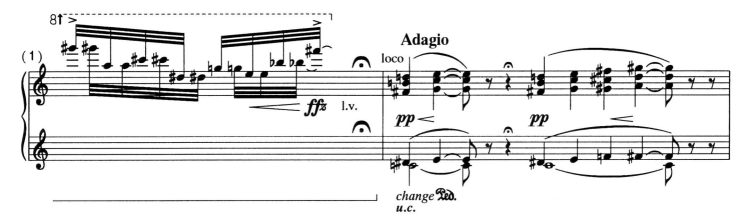

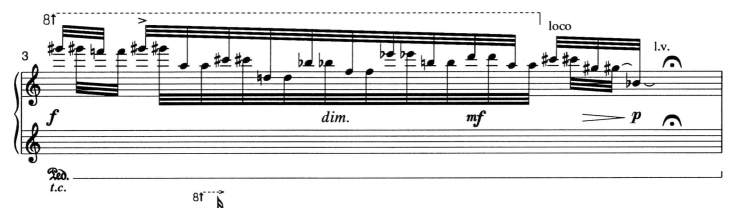

*If it is easier, reverse
hands throughout:

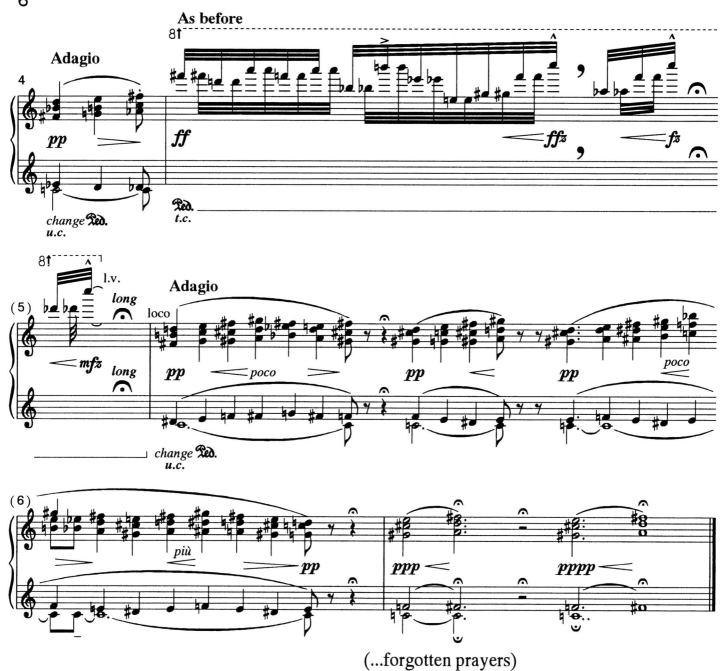

(...forgotten prayers)

IV

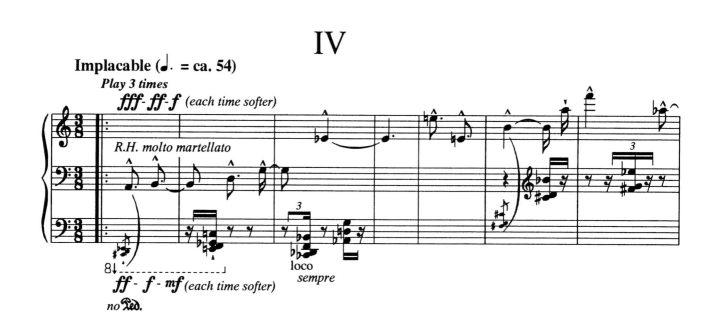

(...cycle de l'univers)

V

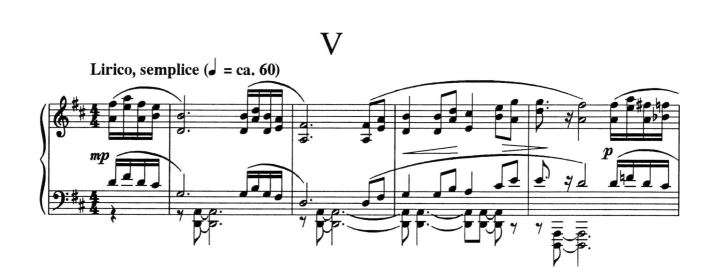

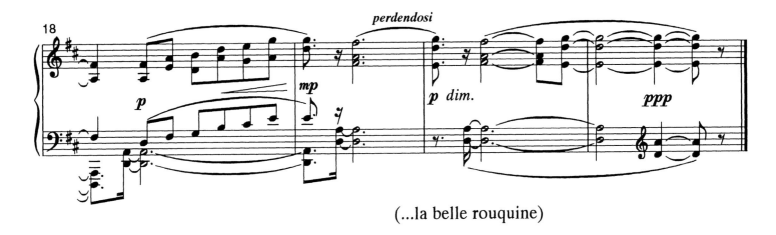

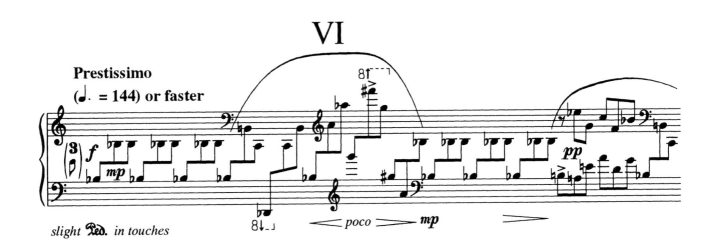

VI

(...la belle rouquine)

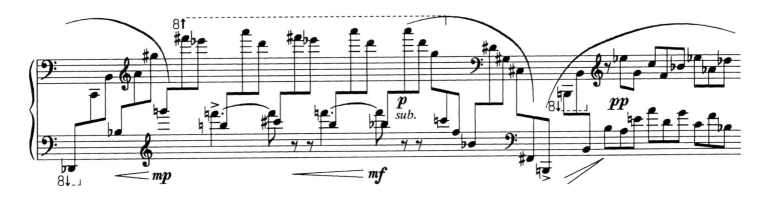

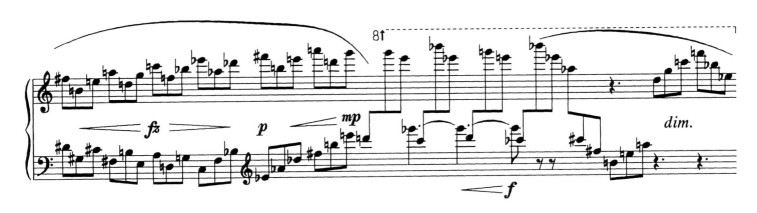

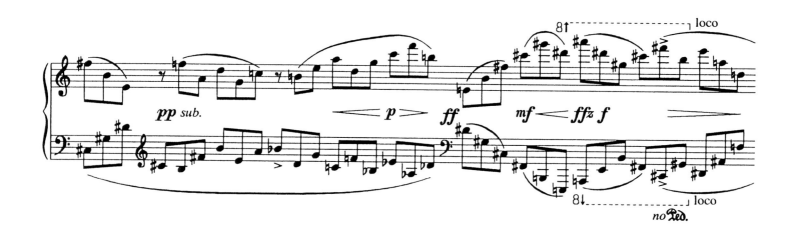

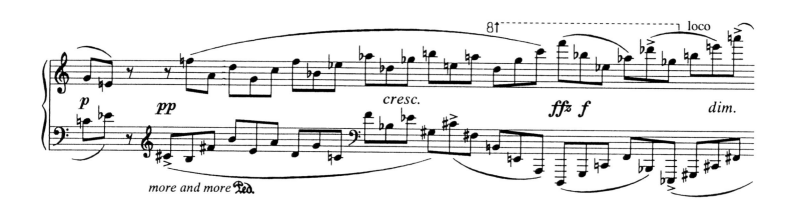

(...Pegasus)

* all notes in cluster between A^1 and D^1

VII

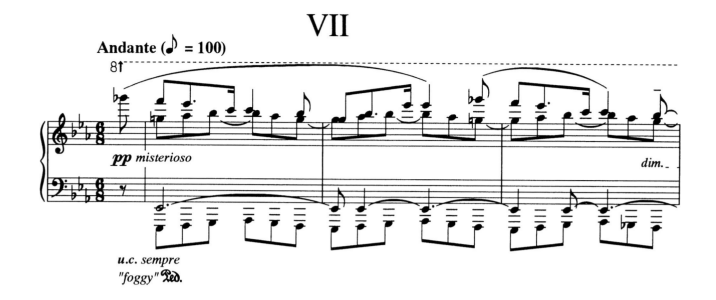

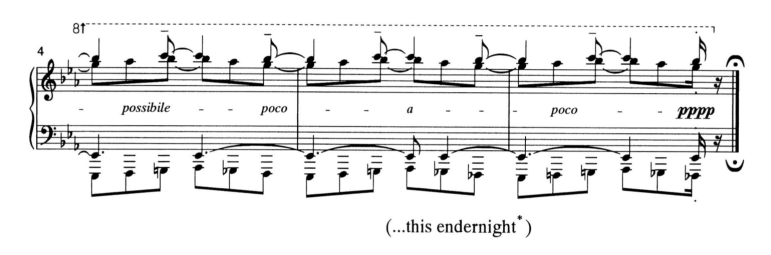

(...this endernight*)

VIII

* **this endernight:** medieval English for "the other night"

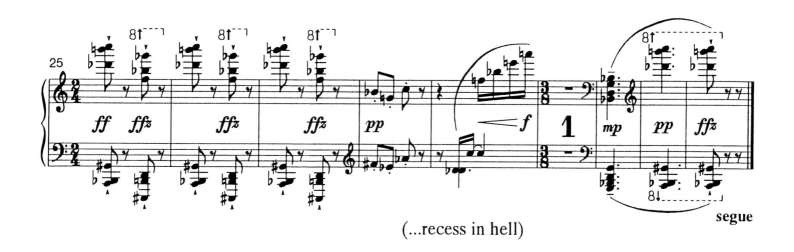

(...recess in hell)

segue

IX

Quick March (♩ = 112 or faster); *in strict time*

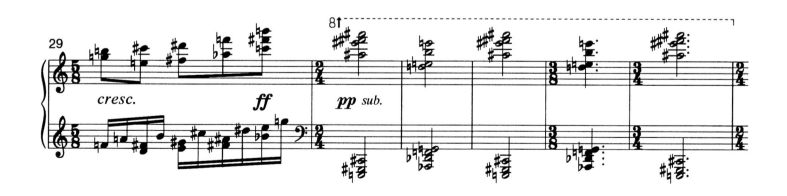

(...Circus Galop)